The Four Quartets

By

T. S. Eliot

Table of Contents

Burnt Norton 3

East Coker 11

The Dry Salvages 22

Little Gidding 33

Burnt Norton

I

Time present and time past
Are both perhaps present in time future
And time future contained in time past.
If all time is eternally present
All time is unredeemable.
What might have been is an abstraction
Remaining a perpetual possibility
Only in a world of speculation.
What might have been and what has been
Point to one end, which is always present.
Footfalls echo in the memory
Down the passage which we did not take
Towards the door we never opened
Into the rose-garden. My words echo
Thus, in your mind.
                    But to what purpose
Disturbing the dust on a bowl of rose-leaves
I do not know.
                    Other echoes
Inhabit the garden. Shall we follow?
Quick, said the bird, find them, find them,
Round the corner. Through the first gate,
Into our first world, shall we follow

The deception of the thrush? Into our first
world.
There they were, dignified, invisible,
Moving without pressure, over the dead leaves,
In the autumn heat, through the vibrant air,
And the bird called, in response to
The unheard music hidden in the shrubbery,
And the unseen eyebeam crossed, for the roses
Had the look of flowers that are looked at.
There they were as our guests, accepted and
accepting.
So we moved, and they, in a formal pattern,
Along the empty alley, into the box circle,
To look down into the drained pool.
Dry the pool, dry concrete, brown edged,
And the pool was filled with water out of
sunlight,
And the lotos rose, quietly, quietly,
The surface glittered out of heart of light,
And they were behind us, reflected in the pool.
Then a cloud passed, and the pool was empty.
Go, said the bird, for the leaves were full of
children,
Hidden excitedly, containing laughter.
Go, go, go, said the bird: human kind
Cannot bear very much reality.
Time past and time future
What might have been and what has been
Point to one end, which is always present.

II

Garlic and sapphires in the mud
Clot the bedded axle-tree.
The trilling wire in the blood
Sings below inveterate scars
Appeasing long forgotten wars.
The dance along the artery
The circulation of the lymph
Are figured in the drift of stars
Ascend to summer in the tree
We move above the moving tree
In light upon the figured leaf
And hear upon the sodden floor
Below, the boarhound and the boar
Pursue their pattern as before
But reconciled among the stars.

At the still point of the turning world. Neither
flesh nor fleshless;
Neither from nor towards; at the still point,
there the dance is,
But neither arrest nor movement. And do not
call it fixity,
Where past and future are gathered. Neither
movement from nor towards,
Neither ascent nor decline. Except for the point,
the still point,
There would be no dance, and there is only the
dance.
I can only say, *there* we have been: but I cannot
say where.
And I cannot say, how long, for that is to place
it in time.

The inner freedom from the practical desire,
The release from action and suffering, release
from the inner
And the outer compulsion, yet surrounded
By a grace of sense, a white light still and
moving,
Erhebung without motion, concentration
Without elimination, both a new world
And the old made explicit, understood
In the completion of its partial ecstasy,
The resolution of its partial horror.
Yet the enchainment of past and future
Woven in the weakness of the changing body,
Protects mankind from heaven and damnation
Which flesh cannot endure.
                              Time past and
time future
Allow but a little consciousness.
To be conscious is not to be in time
But only in time can the moment in the rose-
garden,
The moment in the arbour where the rain beat,
The moment in the draughty church at
smokefall
Be remembered; involved with past and future.
Only through time time is conquered.

III

Here is a place of disaffection
Time before and time after
In a dim light: neither daylight

Investing form with lucid stillness
Turning shadow into transient beauty
Wtih slow rotation suggesting permanence
Nor darkness to purify the soul
Emptying the sensual with deprivation
Cleansing affection from the temporal.
Neither plentitude nor vacancy. Only a flicker
Over the strained time-ridden faces
Distracted from distraction by distraction
Filled with fancies and empty of meaning
Tumid apathy with no concentration
Men and bits of paper, whirled by the cold
wind
That blows before and after time,
Wind in and out of unwholesome lungs
Time before and time after.
Eructation of unhealthy souls
Into the faded air, the torpid
Driven on the wind that sweeps the gloomy
hills of London,
Hampstead and Clerkenwell, Campden and
Putney,
Highgate, Primrose and Ludgate. Not here
Not here the darkness, in this twittering world.

      Descend lower, descend only
Into the world of perpetual solitude,
World not world, but that which is not world,
Internal darkness, deprivation
And destitution of all property,
Dessication of the world of sense,
Evacuation of the world of fancy,

Inoperancy of the world of spirit;
This is the one way, and the other
Is the same, not in movement
But abstention from movememnt; while the
world moves
In appetency, on its metalled ways
Of time past and time future.

IV

Time and the bell have buried the day,
the black cloud carries the sun away.
Will the sunflower turn to us, will the clematis
Stray down, bend to us; tendril and spray
Clutch and cling?
Chill
Fingers of yew be curled
Down on us? After the kingfisher's wing
Has answered light to light, and is silent, the
light is still
At the still point of the turning world.

V

Words move, music moves
Only in time; but that which is only living
Can only die. Words, after speech, reach
Into the silence. Only by the form, the pattern,
Can words or music reach
The stillness, as a Chinese jar still
Moves perpetually in its stillness.
Not the stillness of the violin, while the note

lasts,
Not that only, but the co-existence,
Or say that the end precedes the beginning,
And the end and the beginning were always
there
Before the beginning and after the end.
And all is always now. Words strain,
Crack and sometimes break, under the burden,
Under the tension, slip, slide, perish,
Will not stay still. Shrieking voices
Scolding, mocking, or merely chattering,
Always assail them. The Word in the desert
Is most attacked by voices of temptation,
The crying shadow in the funeral dance,
The loud lament of the disconsolate chimera.

    The detail of the pattern is movement,
As in the figure of the ten stairs.
Desire itself is movement
Not in itself desirable;
Love is itself unmoving,
Only the cause and end of movement,
Timeless, and undesiring
Except in the aspect of time
Caught in the form of limitation
Between un-being and being.
Sudden in a shaft of sunlight
Even while the dust moves
There rises the hidden laughter
Of children in the foliage
Quick now, here, now, always-

Ridiculous the waste sad time
Stretching before and after.

East Coker

I

    In my beginning is my end. In succession
Houses rise and fall, crumble, are extended,
Are removed, destroyed, restored, or in their
place
Is an open field, or a factory, or a by-pass.
Old stone to new building, old timber to new
fires,
Old fires to ashes, and ashes to the earth
Which is already flesh, fur and faeces,
Bone of man and beast, cornstalk and leaf.
Houses live and die: there is a time for building
And a time for living and for generation
And a time for the wind to break the loosened
pane
And to shake the wainscot where the field-
mouse trots
And to shake the tattered arras woven with a
silent motto.

    In my beginning is my end. Now the light
falls

Across the open field,, leaving the deep lane
Shuttered with branches, dark in the afternoon,
Where you lean against a bank while a van
passes,
And the deep lane insists on the direction
Into the village, in the elctric heat
Hypnotised. In a warm haze the sultry light
Is absorbed, not refracted, by grey stone.
The dahlias sleep in the empty silence.
Wait for the early owl.

                    In that open field
If you do not come too close, if you do not come
too close,
On a summer midnight, you can hear the music
Of the weak pipe and the little drum
And see them dancing around the bonfire
the association of man and woman
In daunsinge, signifying matrimonie~
A dignified and commodious sacrament.
Two and two, necessarye coniunction,
Holding eche other by the hand or the arm
Whiche betokeneth concorde. Round and
round the fire
Leaping through the flames, or joined in circles,
Rustically solemn or in rustic laughter
Lifting heavy feet in clumsy shoes,
Earth feet, loam feet, lifted in country mirth
Mirth of those long since under earth
Nourishing the corn. Keeping time,
Keeping the rhythm in their dancing
As in their living in the living seasons

The time of the seasons and the constellations
The time of milking and the time of harvest
The time of the coupling of man and woman
And that of beasts. Feet rising and falling.
Eating and drinking. Dung and death.

    Dawn points, and another day
Prepares for heat and silence. Out at sea the
dawn wind
Wrinkles and slides. I am here
Or there, or elsewhere. In my beginning.

II

What is the late November doing
With the disturbance of the spring
And creatures of the summer heat,
And snowdrops writhing under feet
And hollyhocks that aim too high
Red into grey and tumble down
Late roses filled with early snow?
Thunder rolled by the rolling stars
Simulates triumphal cars
Deployed in constellated wars
Scorpion fights against the Sun
Until the Sun and Moon go down
Comets weep and Leonids fly
Hunt the heavens and the plains
Whirled in a vortex that shall bring
The world to that destructive fire
Which burns before the ice-cap reigns.

 That was a way of putting it - not very
satisfactory:
A periphrastic study in a worn-out poetical
fashion,
Leaving one still with the intolerable wrestle
With words and meanings. The poetry does not
matter.
It was not (to start again) what one had
expected.
What was to be the value of the long looked
forward to,
Long hoped for calm, the autumnal serenity
And the wisdom of age? Had they deceived us,
Or deceived themselves, the quiet-voiced
elders,
Bequeathing us merely a receipt for deceit?
The serenity only a deliberate hebetude,
The wisdom only the knowledge of dead
secrets
Useless in the darkness into which they peered
Or from which they turned their eyes. There is,
it seems to us,
At best, only a limited value
In the knowledge derived from experience.
The knowledge inposes a pattern, and falsifies,
For the pattern is new in every moment
And every moment is a new and shocking
Valuation of all we have been. We are only
undeceived
Of that which, deceiving, could no longer harm.
In the middle, not only in the middle of the way
but all the way, in a dark wood, in a bramble,

On the edge of a grimpen, where is no secure
foothold,
And menaced by monsters, fancy lights,
Risking enchantment. Do not let me hear
Of the wisdom of old men, but rahter of their
folly,
Their fear of fear and frenzy, their fear of
possession,
Of belonging to another, or to others, or to God.
The only wisdom we can hope to acquire
Is the wisdom of humility: humility is endless.

The houses are all gone under the sea.

The dancers are all gone under the hill.

III

O dark dark dark. They all go into the dark,
The vacant interstellar spaces, the vacant into
the vacant,
The captains, merchant bankers, eminent men
of letters,
The generous patrons of art, the statesmen and
the rulers,
Distinguished civil servants, chairmen of many
committees,
Industrial lords and petty contractors, all go
into the dark,
And dark the Sun and Moon, and the
Almanach de Gotha
And the Stock Exchange Gazette, the Directory

of Directors,
And cold the sense and lost the motive of
action.
And we all go with them, into the silent funeral,
Nobody's funeral, for there is no one to bury.
I said to my soul, be still, and let the dark come
upon you
Which shall be the darkness of God. As, in a
theatre,
The lights are extinguished, for the scene to be
changed
With a hollow rumble of wings, with a
movement of darkness on darkness,
And we know that the hills and the trees, the
distant panorama
And the bold imposing facade are all being
rolled away-
Or as, when an underground train, in the tube,
stops too long between stations
And the conversation rises and slowly fades
into silence
And you see behind every face the mental
emptiness deepen
Leaving only the growing terror of nothing to
think about;
Or when, under ether, the mind is conscious
but conscious of nothing-
I said to my soul, be still, and wait without
hope
For hope would be hope for the wrong thing;
wait without love,
For love would be love of the wrong thing;

there is yet faith
But the faith and the love and the hope are all
in the waiting.
Wait without thought, for you are not ready for
thought:
So the darkness shall be the light, and the
stillness the dancing.
Whisper of running streams, and winter
lightning.
The wild thyme unseen and the wild
strawberry,
The laughter in the garden, echoed ecstasy
Not lost, but requiring, pointing to the agony
Of death and birth.

                  You say I am
repeating
Something I have said before. I shall say it
again.
Shall I say it again? In order to arrive there,
To arrive where you are, to get from where you
are not,
     You must go by a way wherein there is no
ecstacy.
In order to arrive at what you do not know
     You must go by a way which is the way of
ignorance.
In order to possess what you do not possess
     You must go by the way of dispossession.
In order to arrive at what you are not
     You must go through the way in which you
are not.

And what you do not know is the only thing
you know
And what you own is what you do not own
And where you are is where you are not.

IV

The wounded surgeon plies the steel
That quesions the distempered part;
Beneath the bleeding hands we feel
The sharp compassion of the healer's art
Resolving the enigma of the fever chart.

Our only health is the disease
If we obey the dying nurse
Whose constant care is not to please
But to remind us of our, and Adam's curse,
And that, to be restored, our sickness must
grow worse.

The whole earth is our hospital
Endowed by the ruined millionaire,
Wherein, if we do well, we shall
Die of the absolute paternal care
That will not leave us, but prevents us
everywhere.

The chill ascends from feet to knees,
The fever sings in mental wires.
If to be warmed, then I must freeze
And quake in frigid purgatorial fires
Of which the flame is roses, and the smoke is
briars.

The dripping blood our only drink,
The bloody flesh our only food:
In spite of which we like to think
That we are sound, substantial flesh and blood-
Again, in spite of that, we call this Friday good.

V

So here I am, in the middle way, having had
twenty years-
Twenty years largely wasted, the years
of *l'entre deux guerres*-
Trying to use words, and every attempt
Is a wholly new start, and a different kind of
failure
Because one has only learnt to get the better of
words
For the thing one no longer has to say, or the
way in which
One is no longer disposed to say it. And so each
venture
Is a new beginning, a raid on the inarticulate,
With shabby equipment always deteriorating
In the general mess of imprecision of feeling,
Undisciplined squads of emotion. And what
there is to conquer
By strength and submission, has already been
discovered
Once or twice, or several times, by men whom
one cannot hope
To emulate - but there is no competition -
There is only the fight to recover what has been

lost
And found and lost again and again: and now,
under conditions
That seem unpropitious. But perhaps neither
gain nor loss.
For us, there is only the trying. The rest is not
our business.

Home is where one starts from. As we grow
older
the world becomes stranger, the pattern more
complicated
Of dead and living. Not the intense moment
Isolated, with no before and after,
But a lifetime burning in every moment
And not the lifetime of one man only
But of old stones that cannot be deciphered.
There is a time for the evening under starlight,
A time for the evening under lamplight
(The evening with the photograph album).
Love is most nearly itself
When here and now cease to matter.
Old men ought to be explorers
Here or there does not matter
We must be still and still moving
Into another intensity
For a further union, a deeper communion
Through the dark cold and the empty
desolation,

The wave cry, the wind cry, the vast waters
Of the petrel and the porpoise. In my end is my
beginning.

The Dry Salvages

(The Dry Salvages - presumably *les trois sauvages* - is a small
group of rocks, with a beacon, off the N.E. coast of Cape Ann,
Massachusetts. *Salvages* is pronounced to rhyme with *assuages*.
Groaner: a whistling buoy.)

I

I do not know much about gods; but I think that the river
Is a strong brown god - sullen, untamed and intractable,
Patient to some degree, at first recognised as a frontier;
Useful, untrustworthy, as a conveyor of commerce;
Then only a problem confronting the builder of bridges.
The problem once solved, the brown god is almost forgotten
By the dwellers in cities - ever, however,

implacable.
Keeping his seasons, and rages, destroyer,
reminder
Of what men choose to forget. Unhonoured,
unpropitiated
By worshippers of the machine, but waiting,
watching and waiting.
His rhythm was present in the nursery
bedroom,
In the rank ailanthus of the April dooryard,
In the smell of grapes on the autumn table,
And the evening circle in the winter gaslight.

     The river is within us, the sea is all about
us;
The sea is the land's edge also, the granite,
Into which it reaches, the beaches where it
tosses
Its hints of earlier and other creation:
The starfish, the horseshoe crab, the whale's
backbone;
The pools where it offers to our curiosity
The more delicate algae and the sea anemone.
It tosses up our losses, the torn seine,
The shattered lobsterpot, the broken oar
And the gear of foreign dead men. The sea has
many voices,
Many gods and many voices.
               The salt is on the
briar rose,
The fog is in the fir trees.
             The sea howl

And the sea yelp, are different voices
Often together heard: the whine in the rigging,
The menace and caress of wave that breaks on
water,
The distant rote in the granite teeth,
And the wailing warning form the approaching
headland
Are all sea voices, and the heaving groaner
Rounded homewards, and the seagull:
And under the oppression of the silent fog
The tolling bell
Measures time not our time, rung by the
unhurried
Ground swell, a time
Older than the time of chronometers, older
Than time counted by anxious worried women
Lying awake, calculating the future,
Trying to unweave, unwind, unravel
And piece together the past and the future,
Between midnight and dawn, when the past is
all deception,
The future futureless, before the morning watch
Whem time stops and time is never ending;
And the ground swell, that is and was from the
beginning,
Clangs
The bell.

II

Where is there an end of it, the soundless
wailing,

The silent withering of autumn flowers
Dropping their petals and remaining
motionless;
Where is there and end to the drifting
wreckage,
The prayer of the bone on the beach, the
unprayable
Prayer at the calamitous annunciation?

There is no end, but addition: the trailing
Consequence of further days and hours,
While emotion takes to itself the emotionless
Years of living among the breakage
Of what was believed in as the most reliable-
And therefore the fittest for renunciation.

There is the final addition, the failing
Pride or resentment at failing powers,
The unattached devotion which might pass for
devotionless,
In a drifting boat with a slow leakage,
The silent listening to the undeniable
Clamour of the bell of the last annunciation.

Where is the end of them, the fishermen
sailing
Into the wind's tail, where the fog cowers?
We cannot think of a time that is oceanless
Or of an ocean not littered with wastage
Or of a future that is not liable
Like the past, to have no destination.

We have to think of them as forever bailing,
Setting and hauling, while the North East
lowers
Over shallow banks unchanging and
erosionless
Or drawing their money, drying sails at
dockage;
Not as making a trip that will be unpayable
For a haul that will not bear examination.

There is no end of it, the voiceless wailing,
No end to the withering of withered flowers,
To the movement of pain that is painless and
motionless,
To the drift of the sea and the drifting
wreckage,
The bone's prayer to Death its God. Only the
hardly, barely prayable
Prayer of the one Annunciation.

It seems, as one becomes older,
That the past has another pattern, and ceases to
be a mere sequence-
Or even development: the latter a partial fallacy
Encouraged by superficial notions of evolution,
Which becomes, in the popular mind, a means
of disowning the past.
The moments of happiness - not the sense of
well-being,
Fruition, fulfilment, security or affecton,
Or even a very good dinner, but the sudden
illumination —

We had the experience but missed the meaning,
And approach to the meaning restores the
experience
In a different form, beyond any meaning
We can assign to happiness. I have said before
That the past experience revived in the
meaning
Is not the experience of one life only
But of many generations - not forgetting
Something that is probably quite ineffable:
The backward look behind the assurance
Of recorded history, the backward half-look
Over the shoulder, towards the primitive terror.
Now, we come to discover that the moments of
agony
(Whether, or not, due to misunderstanding,
Having hoped for the wrong things or dreaded
the wrong things,
Is not in question) are likewise permanent
With such permanence as time has. We
appreciate this better
In the agony of others, nearly experienced,
Involving ourselves, than in our own.
For our own past is covered by the currents of
action,
But the torment of others remains an experience
Unqualified, unworn by subsequent attrition.
People change, and smile: but the agony abides.
Time the destroyer is time the preserver,
Like the river with its cargo of dead negroes,
cows and chicken coops,
The bitter apple, and the bite in the apple.

And the ragged rock in the restless waters,
Waves wash over it, fogs conceal it;
On a halcyon day it is merely a monument,
In navigable weather it is always a seamark
To lay a course by, but in the sombre season
Or the sudden fury, is what it always was.

III

I sometimes wonder if that is what Krishna
meant-
Among other things - or one way of putting the
same thing:
That the future is a faded song, a Royal Rose or
a lavender spray
Of wistful regret for those who are not yet here
to regret,
Pressed between yellow leaves of a book that
has never been opened.
And the way up is the way down, the way
forward is the way back.
You cannot face it steadily, but this thing is
sure,
That time is no healer: the patient is no longer
here.
When the train starts, and the passengers are
settled
To fruit, periodicals and business letters
(And those who saw them off have left the
platform)
Their faces relax from grief into relief,
To the sleepy rhythm of a hundred hours.

Fare forward, travellers! not escaping from the
past
Into different lives, or into any future;
You are not the same people who left that
station
Or who will arrive at any terminus,
While the narrowing rails slide together behind
you;
Watching the furrow that widens behind you,
You shall not think "the past is finished"
Or "the future is before us".
At nightfall, in the rigging and the aerial,
Is a voice descanting (though not to the ear,
The murmuring shell of time, and not in any
language)
"Fare forward, you who think that you are
voyaging;
You are not those who saw the harbour
Receding, or those who will disembark.
Here between the hither and the farther shore
While time is withdrawn, consider the future
And the past with an equal mind.
At the moment which is not of action or
inaction
You can receive this: 'on whatever sphere of
being
The mind of a man may be intent
At the time of death' - that is the one action
(And the time of death is every moment)
Which shall fructify in the lives of others:
And do not think of the fruit of action.
Fare forward.

O voyagers, O seamen,
You who came to port, and you whose bodies
Will suffer the trial and judgement of the sea,
Or whatever event, this is your real
destination."
So Krishna, as when he admonished Arjuna
On the field of battle.

                    Not fare well,
But fare forward, voyagers.

                    IV

    Lady, whose shrine stands on the
promontory,
Pray for all those who are in ships, those
Whose business has to do with fish, and
Those concerned with every lawful traffic
And those who conduct them.

    Repeat a prayer also on behalf of
Women who have seen their sons or husbands
Setting forth, and not returning:
Figlia del tuo figlio,
Queen of Heaven.

    Also pray for those who were in ships, and
Ended their voyage on the sand, in the sea's lips
Or in the dark throat which will not reject them
Or wherever cannot reach them the sound of
the sea bell's
Perpetual angelus.

                    V

To communicate with Mars, converse with
spirits,
To report the behaviour of the sea monster,
Describe the horoscope, haruspicate or scry,
Observe disease in signatures, evoke
Biography from the wrinkles of the palm
And tragedy from fingers; release omens
By sortilege, or tea leaves, riddle the inevitable
With playing cards, fiddle with pentagrams
Or barbituric acids, or dissect
The recurrent image into pre-conscious terrors-
To explore the womb, or tomb, or dreams; all
these are usual
Pastimes and drugs, and features of the press:
And always will be, some of them especially
Whether on the shores of Asia, or in the
Edgware Road,
Men's curiosity searches past and future
And clings to that dimension. But to apprehend
The point of intersection of the timeless
With time, is an occupation for the saint —
No occupation either, but something given
And taken, in a lifetime's death in love,
Ardour and selflessness and self-surrender.
For most of us, there is only the unattended
Moment, the moment in and out of time,
The distraction fit, lost in a shaft of sunlight,
The wild thyme unseen, or the winter lightning
Or the waterfall, or music heard so deeply
That it is not heard at all, but you are the music
While the music lasts. These are only hints and
guesses,

Hints followed by guesses; and the rest
Is prayer, observance, discipline, thought and
action.
The hint half guessed, the gift half understood,
is Incarnation.
Here the impossible union
Of spheres of evidence is actual,
Here the past and future
Are conquered, and reconciled,
Where action were otherwise movement
Of that which is only moved
And has in it no source of movement —
Driven by daemonic, chthonic
Powers. And right action is freedom
From past and future also.
For most of us, this is the aim
Never here to be realised;
Who are only undefeated
Because we have gone on trying;
We, content at the last
If our temporal reversion nourish
(Not too far from the yew-tree)
The life of significant soil.

Little Gidding

I

Midwinter spring is its own season
Sempiternal though sodden towards sundown,
Suspended in time, between pole and tropic.
Whem the short day is brightest, with frost and
fire,
The brief sun flames the ice, on pond and
ditches,
In windless cold that is the heart's heat,
Reflecting in a watery mirror
A glare that is blindness in the early afternoon.
And glow more intense than blaze of branch, or
brazier,
Stirs the dumb spirit: no wind, but pentecostal
fire
In the dark time of the year. Between melting
and freezing
The soul's sap quivers. There is no earth smell
Or smell of living thing. This is the spring time
But not in time's covenant. Now the hedgerow
Is blanched for an hour with transitory blossom
Of snow, a bloom more sudden
Than that of summer, neither budding nor
fading,
Not in the scheme of generation.
Where is the summer, the unimaginable
Zero summer?

If you came this way,
Taking the route you would be likely to take
From the place you would be likely to come
from,
If you came this way in may time, you would
find the hedges
White again, in May, with voluptuary
sweetness.
It would be the same at the end of the journey,
If you came at night like a broken king,
If you came by day not knowing what you
came for,
It would be the same, when you leave the
rough road
And turn behind the pig-sty to the dull facade
And the tombstone. And what you thought you
came for
Is only a shell, a husk of meaning
From which the purpose breaks only when it is
fulfilled
If at all. Either you had no purpose
Or the purpose is beyond the end you figured
And is altered in fulfilment. There are other
places
Which also are the world's end, some at the sea
jaws,
Or over a dark lake, in a desert or a city —
But this is the nearest, in place and time,
Now and in England.

                    If you came this way,
Taking any route, starting from anywhere,

At any time or at any season,
It would always be the same: you would have
to put off
Sense and notion. You are not here to verify,
Instruct yourself, or inform curiosity
Or carry report. You are here to kneel
Where prayer has been valid. And prayer is
more
Than an order of words, the conscious
occupation
Of the praying mind, or the sound of the voice
praying.
And what the dead had no speech for, when
living,
They can tell you, being dead: the
communication
Of the dead is tongued with fire beyond the
language of the living.
Here, the intersection of the timeless moment
Is England and nowhere. Never and always.

II

Ash on an old man's sleeve
Is all the ash the burnt roses leave.
Dust in the air suspended
Marks the place where a story ended.
Dust inbreathed was a house-
The walls, the wainscot and the mouse,
The death of hope and despair,
        This is the death of air.

There are flood and drouth
Over the eyes and in the mouth,
Dead water and dead sand
Contending for the upper hand.
The parched eviscerate soil
Gapes at the vanity of toil,
Laughs without mirth.
     This is the death of earth.

Water and fire succeed
The town, the pasture and the weed.
Water and fire deride
The sacrifice that we denied.
Water and fire shall rot
The marred foundations we forgot,
Of sanctuary and choir.
     This is the death of water and fire.

In the uncertain hour before the morning
    Near the ending of interminable night
    At the recurrent end of the unending
After the dark dove with the flickering tongue
    Had passed below the horizon of his homing
    While the dead leaves still rattled on like tin
Over the asphalt where no other sound was
    Between three districts whence the smoke
arose
    I met one walking, loitering and hurried
As if blown towards me like the metal leaves
    Before the urban dawn wind unresisting.
    And as I fixed upon the down-turned face
That pointed scrutiny with which we challenge

The first-met stranger in the waning dusk
    I caught the sudden look of some dead
master
Whom I had known, forgotten, half recalled
    Both one and many; in the brown baked
features
    The eyes of a familiar compound ghost
Both intimate and unidentifiable.
    So I assumed a double part, and cried
    And heard another's voice cry: "What!
are *you* here?"
Although we were not. I was still the same,
    Knowing myself yet being someone other —
    And he a face still forming; yet the words
sufficed
To compel the recognition they preceded.
    And so, compliant to the common wind,
    Too strange to each other for
misunderstanding,
In concord at this intersection time
    Of meeting nowhere, no before and after,
    We trod the pavement in a dead patrol.
I said: "The wonder that I feel is easy,
    Yet ease is cause of wonder. Therefore speak:
    I may not comprehend, may not remember."
And he: "I am not eager to rehearse
    My thoughts and theory which you have
forgotten.
    These things have served their purpose: let
them be.
So with your own, and pray they be forgiven
    By others, as I pray you to forgive

Both bad and good. Last season's fruit is eaten
And the fullfed beast shall kick the empty pail.
   For last year's words belong to last year's language
   And next year's words await another voice.
But, as the passage now presents no hindrance
   To the spirit unappeased and peregrine
   Between two worlds become much like each other,
So I find words I never thought to speak
   In streets I never thought I should revisit
   When I left my body on a distant shore.
Since our concern was speech, and speech impelled us
   To purify the dialect of the tribe
   And urge the mind to aftersight and foresight,
Let me disclose the gifts reserved for age
   To set a crown upon your lifetime's effort.
   First, the cold fricton of expiring sense
Without enchantment, offering no promise
   But bitter tastelessness of shadow fruit
   As body and sould begin to fall asunder.
Second, the conscious impotence of rage
   At human folly, and the laceration
   Of laughter at what ceases to amuse.
And last, the rending pain of re-enactment
   Of all that you have done, and been; the shame
Of things ill done and done to others' harm
   Which once you took for exercise of virtue.

Then fools' approval stings, and honour
stains.
From wrong to wrong the exasperated spirit
    Proceeds, unless restored by that refining fire
    Where you must move in measure, like a
dancer."
The day was breaking. In the disfigured street
    He left me, with a kind of valediction,
    And faded on the blowing of the horn.

III

There are three conditions which often look
alike
Yet differ completely, flourish in the same
hedgerow:
Attachment to self and to things and to persons,
detachment
From self and from things and from persons;
and, growing between them, indifference
Which resembles the others as death resembles
life,
Being between two lives - unflowering,
between
The live and the dead nettle. This is the use of
memory:
For liberation - not less of love but expanding
Of love beyond desire, and so liberation
From the future as well as the past. Thus, love
of a country
Begins as an attachment to our own field of
action

And comes to find that action of little
importance
Though never indifferent. History may be
servitude,
History may be freedom. See, now they vanish,
The faces and places, with the self which, as it
could, loved them,
To become renewed, transfigured, in another
pattern.
Sin is Behovely, but
All shall be well, and
All manner of thing shall be well.
If I think, again, of this place,
And of people, not wholly commendable,
Of not immediate kin or kindness,
But of some peculiar genius,
All touched by a common genius,
United in the strife which divided them;
If I think of a king at nightfall,
Of three men, and more, on the scaffold
And a few who died forgotten
In other places, here and abroad,
And of one who died blind and quiet,
Why should we celebrate
These dead men more than the dying?
It is not to ring the bell backward
Nor is it an incantation
To summon the spectre of a Rose.
We cannot revive old factions
We cannot restore old policies
Or follow an antique drum.
These men, and those who opposed them

And those whom they opposed
Accept the constitution of silence
And are folded in a single party.
Whatever we inherit from the fortunate
We have taken from the defeated
What they had to leave us - a symbol:
A symbol perfected in death.
And all shall be well and
All manner of thing shall be well
By the purification of the motive
In the ground of our beseeching.

IV

The dove descending breaks the air
With flame of incandescent terror
Of which the tongues declare
The one dischage from sin and error.
The only hope, or else despair
   Lies in the choice of pyre of pyre-
   To be redeemed from fire by fire.

Who then devised the torment? Love.
Love is the unfamiliar Name
Behind the hands that wove
The intolerable shirt of flame
Which human power cannot remove.
   We only live, only suspire
   Consumed by either fire or fire.

V

What we call the beginning is often the end
And to make and end is to make a beginning.
The end is where we start from. And every
phrase
And sentence that is right (where every word is
at home,
Taking its place to support the others,
The word neither diffident nor ostentatious,
An easy commerce of the old and the new,
The common word exact without vulgarity,
The formal word precise but not pedantic,
The complete consort dancing together)
Every phrase and every sentence is an end and
a beginning,
Every poem an epitaph. And any action
Is a step to the block, to the fire, down the sea's
throat
Or to an illegible stone: and that is where we
start.
We die with the dying:
See, they depart, and we go with them.
We are born with the dead:
See, they return, and bring us with them.
The moment of the rose and the moment of the
yew-tree
Are of equal duration. A people without history
Is not redeemed from time, for history is a
pattern
Of timeless moments. So, while the light fails
On a winter's afternoon, in a secluded chapel
History is now and England.

With the drawing of this Love and the voice of
this Calling

We shall not cease from exploration
And the end of all our exploring
Will be to arrive where we started
And know the place for the first time.
Through the unknown, unremembered gate
When the last of earth left to discover
Is that which was the beginning;
At the source of the longest river
The voice of the hidden waterfall
And the children in the apple-tree
Not known, because not looked for
But heard, half-heard, in the stillness
Between two waves of the sea.
Quick now, here, now, always —
A condition of complete simplicity
(Costing not less than everything)
And all shall be well and
All manner of thing shall be well
When the tongues of flames are in-folded
Into the crowned knot of fire
And the fire and the rose are one.

THE END.

Made in the USA
Monee, IL
28 November 2023

47529455R00025